I0159003

Artwork by David Ó Druaidh
Copyright © 2017 by David Ó Druaidh
ISBN 978-1-9999082-0-1

**Please keep this book in a safe place and
out of the reach of inferior breeds!**

For Jasmine

The Gorgeous Gizmo

2006 – 2016

MY ROYAL ADVENTURES

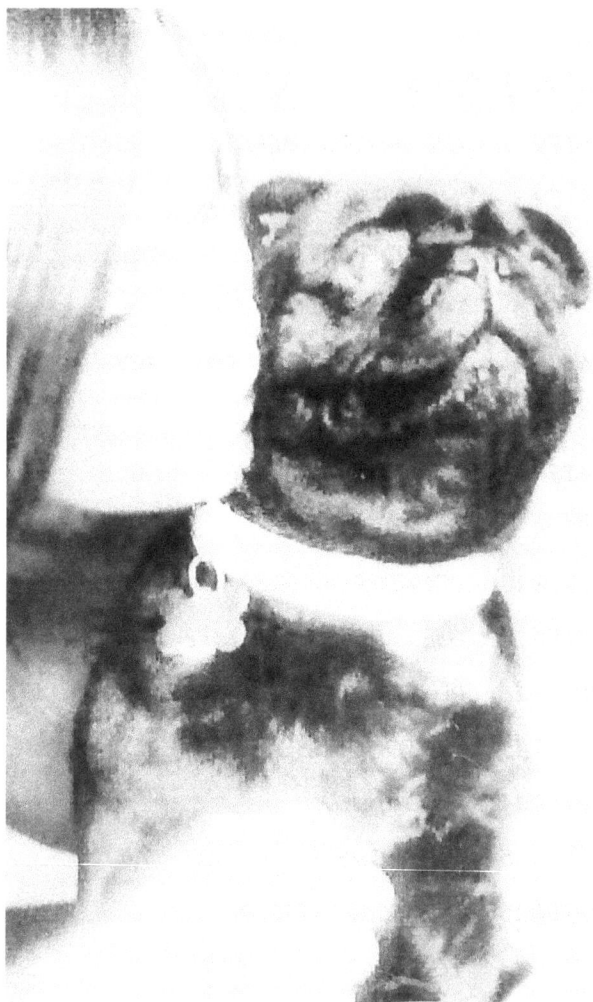

CHAPTER 1

INTRODUCTION

Being the magnificent and public-spirited Pug that I am, I have decided to put paw to keyboard and share some of my thoughts and adventures for your entertainment, education, and edification. A magnanimous gesture on my part, I am sure you will agree.

Let me apologise now if the opening sentence, above, and the remainder of this book for that matter, seems a little wordy. However, try putting yourself in my place. How would you go about capturing a life as rich and varied as mine without a liberal sprinkling of superlatives? (They also call me Garrulous Gizmo, by the way.)

In case you are also wondering if I have swallowed a dictionary, then you are not far wrong. As a matter of fact, I read the latest Oxford edition only last week. While I found the plot disappointing, I nonetheless learned a lot.

Anyway, moving on, the chances are you have chosen this book because you are already a fan, in which case I will need no introduction. Thanks to the internet, of course, my fame has already spread far and wide.

If you are yet to set eyes upon my handsome face, or hear of my fascinating life, you are in for a special treat.

To be honest, I am a little old and tired, so whether you are already a fan or a recent convert, I hope you appreciate my efforts, and the fact that I have taken time out of my hectic schedule for your benefit. The life of a Pug, and a Royal Pug at that, can be very challenging. Between eating, sleeping, and the occasional walk or official visit, there is not much time for anything else. I must confess that I have confined most of my 'official visits' to local restaurants and gastro-pubs of late. International Diplomacy has taken a back seat.

Although they say familiarity breeds contempt, for the purposes of this book you may refer to me as Gizmo, or the Gorgeous Gizmo as I am better known. The reasons for the latter should be obvious enough. For your information, my staff generally refer to me as Sir. On official occasions they refer to me as *Your Pugness* or *Your Royal Pugesty*.

The Latin expression *Multum in Parvo* is oft-used in relation to Pugs. It translates literally as 'much in little'. 'The best things come in small packages' is probably the better-known translation, and it is certainly true in the case of my glorious breed. Moreover, this very motto is incorporated into my family's coat of arms, pictured later in this literary feast.

There is an old joke that probably says a lot about Pugs, too:

Why did the Pug cross the road?
...To get to the better side!

CHAPTER 2

THE ENVIRONMENT

Inevitably, being a high-profile Pug, I am not without my critics. Most of it can safely be put down to jealousy, needless to say.

Some of my detractors have even criticised me for daring to publish this very book, would you believe? Anything I write is sure to fly off the shelves faster than a book about poltergeists, they point out. Imagine the number of trees required to provide the paper!

Let me assuage their fears here and now. In this digital age books can also be transmitted and read electronically without the necessity for sacrificing rain forests. The damage can thus be kept to manageable levels. Furthermore, the enjoyment many will experience reading this book will far outweigh any damage to the planet. Let's get our priorities right.

Never mind global warming. I'm better known for my global charming.

3

Although I might joke about it, in truth my environmental credentials are impeccable. I have turned down no less than three invites to appear on *Top Gear*, including a special edition that was to be themed around dogs. Much as I was tempted to cement my global superstar image by sitting on the famous bench seat beside the engine block table, and leaning forward at the critical moment as everyone always does, I thought better of it. I politely declined because some of the cars they have effectively promoted produce unacceptable emissions.

Rumours that I refused to be seen in a reasonably-priced car are unfounded.

CHAPTER 3

CANINE ROYALTY

As you will no doubt already be aware, Pugs are a Royal Breed. A prestige pedigree, if you like.

While we are known as Pugs in the UK, North America, and much of the rest of the world, we are referred to as Mops in parts of Northern Europe, and Carlins in most of Southern Europe and South America. We have even been called Dutch Bulldogs before now, for reasons which remain obscure. Our closest relatives are actually Mastiffs, would you believe? This may surprise some given their enormity, although they do share our good looks. Perhaps we might, therefore, be thought of as bonsai Mastiffs.

One famous historical Pug fan, Marie Antoinette, called her beloved friend Mopsy, presumably in reference to our Germanic nomenclature, Mops. She is perhaps more famous for having said *"Let them eat cake"*.

This is the traditional interpretation of *"Qu'ils mangent de la brioche,"* which was something about letting the common people taste a little luxury now and again. The truth behind the story, however, is that Mopsy was a little concerned about her weight, and permitted the servants to indulge in some leftover cake after a banquet.

Pugs actually started out on the other side of the world. Back then, China was the greatest civilisation on the planet. It is only fitting, therefore, that this once great empire should produce the greatest ever dog breed. As an acknowledged Royal breed, only Emperors and selected aristocracy were permitted to possess a Pug. The only peasants to come into contact with us were our adoring servants, and what a privileged position this must have been. Imagine being a working person back in Dynastic days. Your friends and family might have been mere bankers, farmers, or medical practitioners, but you got to boast about working with Pugs. It would be like winning the lottery today.

How things have changed, and not always for the better. Today, it is possible for members of the general public to purchase a Pug, albeit for a price from select breeders. Fortunately, the hoi polloi tend to go for more aggressive breeds, so the type of person who is prepared to dedicate themselves to a Pug tends to be a cut above your average Joe.

For example, I was looking over a friend's shoulder the other day as they browsed puppies on the internet, while making *"Ahhh, so cute,"* kind of noises. Various dog breeds were going for differing sums of money when an advertisement for Pug puppies caught my eye. It stood out from the rest. It didn't mention a price, but merely stated that a loving home was required. Clearly, money is not the motivating factor for Pug lovers. Then again, if you have to ask the price, you probably can't afford one. It is flattering, all the same, to think that a select few are prepared to pay for the privilege of serving us.

CHAPTER 4

LOOKING BACK

I began life in Gillingham, a Medway town South East of London, in the UK. It's not such a bad place to start out, but I soon moved on to better things.

I was sleeping with my family one day when a young girl, Jasmine, came to visit. She was accompanied by her father, Ashley, who chatted with my housekeeper, and offered a large sum of money in return for the privilege of my companionship. I Soon found myself being driven in a large car. A Rolls Royce would have been preferable, but I made do with a Mercedes as Jasmine was very sweet, and Ashley drove carefully. Jasmine was only twelve years old at the time so, clearly, she was in need of a guiding light, and I was happy to oblige. I decided to adopt her as a kind of pet project, if you will pardon the pun.

My father had taken a shine to Ashley, and offered him a small cuddly toy as token of friendship. Ashley noticed that my father was missing an eye, and immediately offered his sympathy. His eye had been taken out, unfortunately, in a vicious and unprovoked attack by a local cat. So many people labour under the misapprehension that dogs are the aggressors in the great dog-cat divide, but in truth cats are generally the mischief makers. Sadly, this misconception is all too often perpetuated by a complaisant mainstream media.

Because many in the media work long hours, they prefer to keep cats. Most of them have been brainwashed, in other words. I have even seen television cartoons where dogs chase cats purely out of spite. Such a ridiculous notion defies serious contemplation.

Very soon the car arrived in Purley. By now I had fallen asleep in Jasmine's lap, only to be woken by the car slowing to a halt on a slightly inclined driveway, which lead to a rather grand house surrounded by tall trees. A gardener laboured on the front lawn, and a delivery man ran down the steps with a large package. A tall blonde woman greeted us at the doorway. The lady was called Rebecca, and she spoke a strange foreign language that sounded very much like that spoken by the crazy chef on the Muppet show. I met this famous chef once, after I was approached to appear on a special edition of the same television show. Naturally, I declined. Well, by way of analogy, can you imagine the Queen of England making a cameo appearance on, say, the Jeremy Kyle show, or being interviewed by Piers Morgan? A little beneath her dignity, shall we say, let alone mine.

Anyway, it turned out that Rebecca was Jasmine's mother, and she was Norwegian. She didn't seem very keen on me at first but, inevitably, she soon warmed to my charm and good looks. This saved the inconvenience of all the paperwork involved in dismissing a member of staff. Rebecca will probably never know how close she came to living in the woods behind the house.

I was beginning to feel quite at home already. The house resembled some of the palaces from my previous lives, and there was clearly no shortage of people available to wait on me. In view of the satisfactory nature of these new surrounds, I sent a message to my family back in Gillingham. It went something like this: *Don't expect me back any time soon, thanks for all the food, and stay in touch.*

CHAPTER 5

THE HOUSE ON

THE HILL

My new surrounds were perfect. The house was in Purley, South East London, and it sported grand entrance gates. It was situated atop a hill, and commanded panoramic views over the lowlands and the neat rows of terraced houses provided for working class people. The kind of people who serve Pugs and the industries that have grown up around us, in other words.

A tall man by the name of David was appointed my Butler and personal bodyguard. He did a pretty good job, although his favoured watering hole was not to my taste. I would have preferred somewhere a little more recherché.

Providing the weather was clement, and it wasn't too busy, he would often walk me around the gardens next to it, where occasionally people would bow to me and talk to David. It was only polite, of course, that communications were conveyed via him. I would generally ignore people unless they spoke to him first. Protocol and all that. I sometimes referred to David as my dogsbody, but not when he was in earshot. Others in the household called him Shrek, but likewise not to his face. (Coincidentally, David hails from the county of Worcestershire in the UK, which is mentioned in the film that the real Shrek appears in.)

On one occasion he left me sleeping in one of my fur-lined baskets in his Mercedes, just outside the entrance to the public house in question. Well, we all need our beauty sleep, and especially me in view of my surplus of riches in this department. Unfortunately, I was spotted by a German tourist, and before I knew it the whole car was surrounded by a group of them making patronising sounds as if I was an animal in a zoo.

Fortunately, David was quick to come to my rescue, or so I thought. Instead of driving me away, however, the next thing I knew I was outside the car and posing for photographs with them. Tut. The things I am prepared to tolerate in order to prevent another war!

To be honest, I suspect David is not averse to taking the odd backhander, as if being my personal minder is not reward enough. Still, I suppose it is only fair that he avails himself of the opportunity to supplement his meagre stipend now and again in view of the importance of his calling.

CHAPTER 6

INTERNATIONAL DIPLOMACY

I generally restrict my travels to countries with strong Royal connections. Spain, Norway, and Holland, are acceptable, for example. I have driven through France — very quickly — but I prefer not to stop in view of their brutal history. They chopped the heads of their Royalty, remember, which begs the question: who was left to look after the Pugs? I have not heard of any Pugs losing their heads, but who knows for sure what really went on. After all, the French eat horses! Is nothing beneath them? I prefer Chicken, personally.

Ironically, I do happen to be fluent in French, but not because I am a big fan of their culture, although much of their food and wine does meet with my approval. Au Contraire. I do so because French used to be the language of international diplomacy. In fact, the French still refer to their mother tongue as the Language of Kings, although I think that is a bit of a stretch to be honest, not least in view of their grotesque penchant for the guillotine.

Two of my favourite places on this little planet are the island of Mallorca in Spain (pronounced Majorca for non-Spanish speakers), where their King often sojourns, and Oslo in Norway. Mallorca is pleasant and mild in the winter months, and Oslo not too hot in the summer months. Travelling between the two, when not in London, saves my staff having to bathe me every day. After all, they need time to relax, too. Tired and stressed staff are less efficient in my experience.

I am yet to meet the King of Spain. The trouble is, he likes to spend time on his yacht, and I'm not the best on water. As for the Queen of England, suffice to say that I have politely declined her overtures thus far. Few people realise that Corgis were originally cattle dogs! Until they go, I don't. I won't be making any official visits until then. I have standards to keep, even if she doesn't.

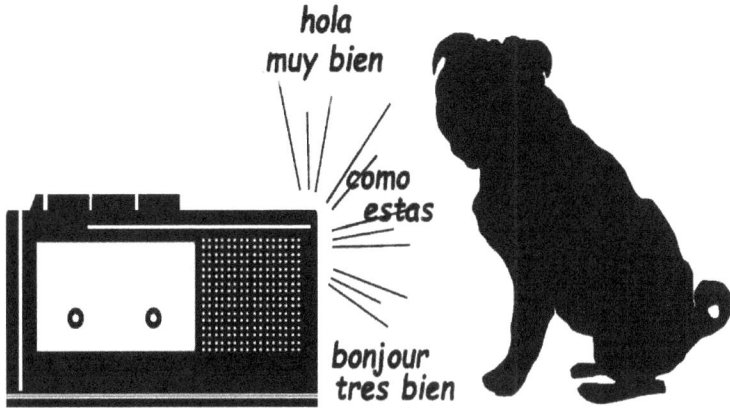

CHAPTER 7

THE LANGUAGE

BARRIER

On one occasion the gardener at the house in Purley picked me up and held me in the palm of his hand. Well, he was a big man. Almost as big as David, my butler. He looked me in the eye, and said: *"It doesn't get much worse than that!"*

I was horrified, at first, and demanded that David fire him, immediately. David took me aside and said: *"Look boss. He's very good, and he's cheap."* David also went on to try and convince me that it was really a veiled compliment, explaining that there was only one thing worse than being talked about, and that was not being talked about. I was less than convinced, but David went on.

13

"I think something has been lost in translation," he said. "In America, for example, when they say 'bad', they mean 'good'."

I was beginning to think David should be working in international diplomacy, but I didn't mention it in case he demanded a pay rise. I let this assault on my dignity pass. Consider it a mark of my class.

CHAPTER 8

A WALK IN

THE PARK

Much as I enjoy a walk in the park, they can be stressful on occasion. All too often I have to defend my care staff from the unwanted attentions of other canines, jealous of my prestige pedigree, position, and the splendid house provided for my comfort. The walks are good exercise for my staff, so I try to take them out regularly, albeit on the other end of a leash lest they get lost in some of the woodland surrounding the house, or walk into the road. Many cars drive too fast through the neighbourhood, presumably because most of its inhabitants can afford the prestige marques that typically come with large engines as standard. More money than sense, you might say.

My personal butler, David, generally assumes responsibility for my exercise program. I like to walk twice a day. Trouble is, being a tall man, David's idea of a walk is sometimes more of a marathon for me. It helps keep us both in good shape, so I shouldn't complain, and the bigger and stronger he is, the better able he is to carry me when necessary, such as at the local post office where the floor is dirty. I certainly wouldn't tolerate being left outside.

(As crazy as that might sound, I have seen dogs tied to the lamp post outside this very location, although only inferior breeds, admittedly. You know, the type that bark and sniff more than is strictly necessary.)

David wasn't the easiest to train, I'm afraid. He was a challenge to begin with, to say the least. On one occasion he threw a stick and looked at me as if I was supposed to run after it. The big dumb animal. He even shouted *"Fetch!"* Can you believe that? I'm a princely Pug, not a park warden employed to clear up detritus. Some of the things I have had to put up with you would not believe.

CHAPTER 9

PICNIC POUR MOI?

Just as David and I entered the park one pleasant evening, my nose twitched and I looked up to see two people sitting on the grass. With the sun behind them, it was difficult to make out their features, silhouetted as they were. Approaching, I realised that there was food on the blanket beside them. What a pleasant surprise! Well, I was feeling a little peckish, and eating indoors most of the time is no challenge. The occasional outdoor snack brings out the wolf in me, and my female admirers love that.

I tucked right in. While I was concentrating on eating, though, I failed to notice that these people didn't belong to my usual entourage. In fact, they were complete strangers, and for some reason they seemed to find it amusing that I was eating the food, which they claimed hadn't been prepared for my benefit.

I felt a little embarrassed, despite the fact it was my land, so I left David to speak with them and put them straight on a few matters. Strangely, he seemed to be apologising. Why? I hadn't given them permission to eat there. I was prepared to forgive them in view of the quality of the food, though. Some of it was mouth-watering. Discretion being the better part of valour, I left the food and went on my way, trusting that David would smooth things over, and make them aware that written permission would be required in future. In view of the delicious sausage rolls, it seemed that a Royal Pardon was in order on this occasion. I let the matter slide.

No 1

CHAPTER 10

LOOKING AFTER NUMBER ONE

I have laid down a few simple rules for my staff:

1. Feed me just twice a day. (I could easily eat more, but I have to think of my waistline and good looks.)

2. Keep the garden free of foxes, cats, and squirrels.

3. Keep my clothes and collars clean, pressed, and ironed.

4. Keep the grass short. That way I am less likely to step in any hidden nasties.

5. Pick up my pooh after me, and dispose of it carefully in the bags provided. I don't want people collecting it and selling it on eBay just because I'm famous. Perish the thought. It is a sad fact that many dogs and humans lead desperate and vicarious lives.

I don't usually have to say much in respect of the house, which is normally kept in good order. Almost every day it is a hive of activity. Washing machines whir, vacuum cleaners hum, and people buzz around me.

Conditions are most satisfactory. I am provided with a selection of comfortable baskets to suit my mood. This also offers the additional convenience of alternatives should any of them be taken away for external cleaning.

By way of happy coincidence, the local laundry is run by a Chinese family who, naturally, understand the strict requirements of my breed.

I am blessed with a number of doting staff. They are not without their shortfalls — they are only human after all — but the weaknesses in some are adequately compensated by the strengths in others.

CHAPTER 11

THE LADIES IN

MY LIFE

You probably won't be surprised to learn that I am not short of female admirers, some of whom travel far and wide for an audience with me. I don't have time to read all my post, sadly, so my staff read me selected highlights. Every day they have to throw masses of it away. They sometimes refer to this as junk mail so as not to embarrass me, but I'm not stupid. I might live a pampered and protected life, but there is no doubting that the vast majority of it is fan mail.

Sadly, some people take the liberty of walking down the steps to the house and poking newspapers through the letter box just to try and get a glimpse of me. I am not averse to the occasional bark to see them off, as inelegant as this might seem. To be fair to the people that stoop to such behaviour, they are probably put up to it by some of the amorous bitches who live locally. C'est la vie.

My live in Concubines are called Maja and Gemma. The latter is spelled with a G in honour of my name beginning with same. I won't bore you with any more details about them. Suffice to say that they are both pretty and they keep me happy. Don't get me wrong. I'm no sexist, but with the exception of Royal circles, the female of the species is lesser than the male. Nature is hierarchical, even if we do refer to her as Mother Nature.

There are exceptions to this rule, of course, such as the Queen of England, but between you and me, British Royalty are considered below par by those in the know. Consider Her Majesty's choice of dog breed, for example.

CHAPTER 12

RUBBING SHOULDERS WITH NOBILITY

Being a select breed, it probably goes without saying that we have enjoyed many famous and aristocratic housekeepers, not to mention royalty. I can think of a few off the top of my head.

Mary Antionette had a Pug called Mopsy, no doubt a play on the Germanic word for our breed, Mops, as already mentioned. Mary Antionette, much like most of the British Royalty, had strong German connections.

William of Orange was saved by his Pug when an assassin crept up on his tent beside the battlefield one night. This heroic Pug woke him and the day was saved. What kind of world would be living in today if William hadn't liberated us from less progressive regimes?

Queen Victoria also preferred Pugs, and there are many more.

Voltaire, the French writer and philosopher; Sammy Davis Junior, the singer-songwriter; Andy Warhol, the pop artist; Grace Kelly, the famous actress and Princess of Monaco; George Clooney, the actor; and Valentino, the famous designer. The roll call of rich and famous Pug lovers is almost as long as the list of distinguished Pugs.

Don't get me wrong. I'm certainly no name-dropper, but I think it's important to give credit to humans where appropriate, and not just their Pug superiors.

CHAPTER 13

RIOTOUS ASSEMBLY

I was taking a stroll in Purley with a staff member one evening when we spotted a sign on the wall of a local church. **'Dog Training Tonight 7pm'**. As it happened, it had just turned seven, so I thought I'd pop in to take a look, and perhaps offer my advice. Sadly, the scene was one of chaos and disorder, with far too many intemperate breeds barking, growling, and generally misbehaving. No sooner I walked in than they turned on me, one to a dog. Jealousy soon got the better of these inferior creatures.

I'm not sure whether it was my pearl encrusted collar, or my superior bearing. Whatever the case, I made a mental note to avoid the event in future. Much as I was tempted to bark back, I considered it beneath my dignity, and signalled my disapproval with a disdainful growl.

After consulting with the dog trainer, it was agreed that my attendance was unwise in view of some of the lower castes in situ, and we beat a hasty retreat.

As we walked home, I considered making a call to Robbie, a friend of the family in a nearby village. Robbie was in possession of another fine breed of dog, an Irish Wolfhound called Dufus. He was as big as a horse, but gentle and intelligent with it. He would make a fine minder, in addition to my butler, David, and would no doubt consider it a privilege to look out for me.

Difficult times call for drastic measures, as they say. There was no doubting that some of the locals had it in for me, so precautions might be worth considering. The last time I saw Dufus was on a hunting trip, but given that the hunter had now become the hunted, so to speak, it seemed strangely appropriate, not to mention ironic, that a hunting companion might become my minder.

I could also call on my cousin Patrick from Dublin. Trouble is, being a former boxing champion, this particularly pugnacious Pug is better known for starting trouble than preventing it! He's not a Pug to pull his punches, in other words, and one always has to be careful not to be seen as the aggressor in these matters.

Flight Arrivals
Lane - 1 Barcelona ES1442
Lane - 2 New York DY1307
Lane - 3 London BA1284

CHAPTER 14

FLYING HIGH

I prefer to travel first class when available. This is not always possible, however, especially on some shorter European flights. As if to add insult to injury, on one occasion I was not even permitted to travel in the cabin with my staff. I was caged and placed in the cargo hold. Imagine the humiliation. Although this accommodation was spacious and warm, and I had my own large luxury cage, I nonetheless had to share the cargo area with inferior dog breeds, and even one cat! One of the other dogs, a Staffordshire Bull Terrier I think it was, attempted to strike up conversation with me. His name was Bruno, as I recall. How common. Normally, I would refer any small talk to my human staff, but they were not available as they were forced to fly without me.

The experience was too horrible for words. All this sub-species had to talk about was fighting; about how many other dogs he had bitten, and how many foxes he had chased. It was difficult to know how to respond to such ghastly gibbering. I think I said something like, *"Really, how interesting,"* before I turned away and pretended to fall asleep.

The flight went smoothly enough, but the ground experience was less than dignifying. I was off-loaded with the suitcases, and my cage was transported to the terminal building on the back of a trailer which was towed by a tractor. I was beginning to feel like a farm animal. As if that wasn't bad enough, it was a cold and rainy day, and sometimes the wind blew the rain through the side of my cage. I sat there and shivered. Just lie back and think of England, I thought to myself. This can't last for long.

Fortunately, I soon found myself in a warm terminal building, where I was loaded onto a conveyor belt along with the suitcases. I could have sworn I heard one of the ground crew refer to me as an ugly little critter, although he might have been referring to the awful fake crocodile-skin bag beside me. Otherwise, I'd have had my personal minders report him to the management for summary dismissal. Sadly, long gone are the days when I could have had him hung with a mere motion of my paw.

Due to another careless oversight by airport staff, the door of my cage sprang open. There I was, exposed to the world. Vulnerable. Another dog could have entered my cage for small talk, sniffing, or perhaps worse. (I have had other dogs take a nip at me before now.) I decided to be pro-active. I exited my cage to stretch my legs, before assuming a lofty position on the conveyor belt. On top of a luxury brand of bag, no less, as befitting my status.

As the conveyor belt entered an area populated by humans, presumably waiting to collect their luggage, I was greeted by much pointing and laughter. It seemed the sight of a Royal breed suffering humiliation in this manner was amusing to the peasants. I swallowed my pride and awaited rescue. My staff arrived in due course and I was hurried to a waiting limousine, shaken but not stirred.

CHAPTER 15

MAD DOGS AND ENGLISHMEN

Englishmen have been known to be eccentric, hence the expression, 'Mad Dogs and Englishmen'. The English are not the only eccentric race in Europe, mind you, let alone the world. Annual Pug races are held in Berlin, Germany, would you believe? At first, I was less than impressed by the prospect of my Royal breed being paraded for the amusement of the general public, but I have since warmed to it.

A team of PR consultants originally dreamt up the idea in order to show our playful side. Apparently, we were regarded as aloof and unapproachable in some circles, so an image makeover was deemed appropriate.

A similar tactic was employed by British Royalty a few years ago, and proved successful. A series of events were opened to the general public in order to celebrate Her Royal Highness Queen Elizabeth II, on some anniversary or other, and they were held in the vicinity of Buckingham Palace. My favourite rock band, Queen, played for Her Majesty, and even performed a fine rendition of God Save the Queen. In view of its unexpected success, I felt a little embarrassed to have turned down her invite, but I was in Spain on other business. One can't be in two places at once.

NB. It is a little-known fact that the rock band, Queen, originally wanted to call themselves King, but they were advised against it by none other than my cousin, King Nico the III, another royal Pug and confidante who resides in Cheltenham, Gloucestershire. There was only room for one King in England, as far as he was concerned. The rock band eventually settled for their second-choice name, Queen.

Anyway, the Saturday of this weekend sticks in my mind. Jasmine's father, Ashley, took me for a walk in Puerto Portals, the luxury Marina in Mallorca, Balearic Islands. The very location where King Juan Carlos often moors his yacht, Fortuna. It wasn't there on this particular day, however, as presumably my staff had overlooked to notify him of my visit. We strolled along the pier admiring other luxury yachts, nonetheless. The conditions were perfect. With the sky a little overcast, I enjoyed the relative cool as I can quickly overheat in direct sunlight, especially after a Gin and Tonic or two.

Unfortunately, a little later the clouds separated, the sun beat down, and the temperature quickly soared. Poor old Ashley ended up carrying me home, whereupon we both collapsed in a pool of perspiration. Hence the full and correct expression — *Only Mad Dogs and Englishmen Go Out in The Midday Sun.*

CHAPTER 16

THE 'COMPETITION'

In truth, we have no rivals, but let us consider some other popular breeds, much as it pains me to acknowledge the underclass.

Don't get me started on Yorkshire Terriers, Golden Retrievers, or my bête noire, Labradors. The former are yappy little critters, and the latter over rated. The Labrador family are rumoured to be the best-selling dogs in the world. Still, popularity is rarely a reflection of quality. I would rather listen to classical music than your average pop song, by way of example.

Let me tell you a story about a local black Labrador that tried to attack me. Fortunately, my butler was there to intervene. He simply placed me on his shoulder and out of its reach. The owners of the Labrador, who were understandably embarrassed, took it to a dog psychologist in the hope of gaining some insight into its irrational behaviour. The dog psychologist concluded that my breathing was the problem, though!

Can you believe that? What a nerve. Was this shrink seriously suggesting that the abominable creature ran a few hundred yards across a park to attack me because I'm a heavy breather. The audacity. I'm as fit as a fiddle, and I don't even smoke. (I leave that to beagles.) Well, they send these things to test us, as they say, and my butler certainly passed this test with flying colours. He saved me from having to take a chunk out of the demented Labrador in order to teach it a lesson, and I'm guessing they don't taste very nice.

News has just reached me that French Bull Dogs are now the best-selling breed in the UK! On the plus they look a bit like us, but in truth they're inferior imposters. They are, in fact, only *part* Pug, and that's the problem. Furthermore, they are unable to breed naturally, as male 'Frenchies' are normally too clumsy to mount their female counterparts. How pathetic. Male Pugs, meanwhile, are renowned paramours. Take me for example. I often say, *"I'm a lover, not a fighter."* Not that it is really necessary to reinforce the prowess of a Pug. What's more, Frenchies are notoriously lazy, and prefer not to walk very far. I guess their popularity reflects the decline in public health generally, what with too many obese people now populating the UK.

Opinions vary in respect of King Charles Spaniels. Personally, I think they are little more than pretenders to the throne, but everyone else seems to like them. Being a genuine royal bloodline, it takes more than the word King to fool me, of course. Unfortunately for their fan club, at the end of the day my opinion is the only one that counts.

PUGS IN BLACK

CHAPTER 17

TOO MUCH OF A GOOD THING?

Just as you might have thought the profile of my glorious breed couldn't get any higher, along comes another blockbuster movie featuring Pugs in the leading roles, and with big names like Will Smith and Tommy Lee Jones as supporting actors. On my advice, the director gave Smith and Jones more lines, but there was no mistaking the fact that Pugs were the brains behind the operation — the real Masters of the Universe.

In recent years, the mere mention of my breed will prompt many people to say something like: "*Men in Black, I loved that film, the Pugs were so cute,*" and so on. Occasionally, Will Smith and Tommy Lee Jones will also be credited for their fine performances, overshadowed though they were.

Had it not been for my intervention, mind you, some foolish Hollywood types were about to cast Chihuahuas in the role of the secret rulers of the universe. Imagine that! What kind of brains could you get into those tiny skulls? This would never have worked, needless to say, especially given that Pugs are recognised as the most intelligent and handsome breed this side of Sirius, which, coincidentally, is also known as the Dog Star.

In fairness to the producers, they did at least seem to recognise that Black Pugs are a cut above our fawn and grey coloured brothers and sisters. God moves in mysterious ways, as they say, but this is clearly what he intended.

As God's chosen Pugs, we have not always had the easiest of times. In Franco's Spain, for example, black Pugs were often put to death at birth, doubtless because Franco regarded our superior intellects as a threat to his fascist regime.

My cousin Edgar who lives in Mallorca was so moved by these tragic historical events that he penned the now famous song, 'Is it cos I'm black?' This charted a number of years later when it was covered by a group of singers and musicians who referred to themselves as Rappers. Presumably, this is some form of musical genre?

This reminds me of a very bad joke my chauffeur made the other day. As we were driving through a small town, he pointed to a picture of Pug puppies in the window of a veterinary practice. This particular vet was located between an optician and a bakery. "*Specs, and Pugs, and Sausage Rolls,*" he quipped.

CHAPTER 18

ALL BITE AND
NO BARK

Please do not think I would ever allow power to go my head. Privileged Pug I may be, but I am nonetheless prepared to muck in and do my bit when it counts. Despite having the whole house at my disposal, I very often choose to sleep in the kitchen in order to guard this most strategic of locations. It might not be the most comfortable room in the house, but who could deny it's importance? An army marches on its stomach, as they say, so we would all be in trouble if my army of assistants were to go hungry.

Few people in the house even realise the potential dangers that lurk outside. Many an evening I have spotted a sly fox peeping through the glass of the kitchen door. Eyeing me jealously, and the food laden fridge and cupboards covetously. A growl is usually enough to see them off, even when they appear in numbers. I dare not bark for fear of waking my assistants and, as I have already made clear, tired staff are less efficient staff.

It is occasionally said of me that I am all bite and no bark. Another fitting testimony, I feel. By way of human analogy, you might say that I speak softly and carry a big stick.

MULTUM IN PARVO

CHAPTER 19

GEORGE AND THE DRAGON

Myths and legends very often preserve historical truths, but sometimes the details are lost over time. Being of Chinese origin, Pugs are skilled in the art of Dragon handling. It's in our blood, and dragons form part of our culture, as you are no doubt aware. Today, dragons only survive in remote parts of the world. Very few people ever get to see them, which is a shame as they are beautiful beasts. A few centuries ago, however, dragons were far more commonplace, and were regularly spotted the world over. Back then, there were few if any aircraft in the skies, which pose a threat to dragons today much as cars pose a risk to wild animals like Deer on the roads. Indeed, the fear of mid-air collisions is the main reason why they choose to hide in remote locations nowadays.

Although they are shy and intelligent beasts for the most part, dragons did occasionally go bad back in the day. It was not unknown for them to steal farm animals and burn down wooden buildings with their fiery breath. When this happened, Pugs were normally called in to mediate and, if necessary, arrange for transportation of the dragon in question back to China for psychological evaluation. Very rarely, a champion Pug might be called in to slay a dragon if the beast was deemed beyond rehabilitation.

Perhaps the most famous dragon slayer was George, a Pug ancestor of mine from many centuries ago. Back then, a rogue dragon was creating havoc near Hereford on the English-Welsh border. The dragon tended to hide out in the Welsh mountains, and attack farm animals over the border in England. The Welsh were happy enough with this arrangement, and the dragon in question had no desire to upset the Welsh given that they sported a splendid red dragon on their national flag. George travelled all the way from China to lend his expertise, and resolved the problem with his trusty sword within a few days of arrival. The locals were most grateful, and in the light of their hospitality he decided to settle in England. The fact that he fell for the charms of a local Pug, Gertrude, no doubt had something to do with his decision to stay. They had four puppies together and lived happily ever after.

Sadly, however, the truth has been lost in the telling, and today it is erroneously assumed that George the Dragon Slayer was a swashbuckling knight. In truth he was a princely black Pug, handsome and brave, much like me. To this very day a dragon features on my family coat of arms, pictured above this chapter heading.

Recently, a bunch of Dragons with a Den somewhere in England (something to do with a TV program called Dragons Den, apparently) offered fifty thousand pounds just to spend some time with me, or for a share in my company, or something like that. I was very flattered, but I gave the idea short shrift as I consider capitalism rather vulgar.

CHAPTER 20

PUGS NOT DRUGS

Life can be tough. Despite being an aristocrat myself, I understand that life is not always easy on the working classes. My chauffeur has driven me past some of the little houses they live in. There is not enough space to swing a cat in most of them and, believe me, I'm very much in favour of swinging cats by their tails. The horrible creatures. It would be an Olympic sport if I had my way! Despite numerous sensible proposals to various sporting bodies, however, I am sad to report that the RSPCA have thus far been less than co-operative. In fact, my legal team have described them as deliberately obstructive.

Anyway, getting back to the point, the biggest problem the working classes face in this day-and-age is a lack of leadership and spiritual guidance. Back in Dynastic days, people knew their places, and considered it a privilege — indeed an honour — to serve Pugs. Today there are simply not enough Pugs to go around, and some people who should know better choose to live with inferior breeds. I don't like to harp on about the Queen of England ... but Corgis? Really! As I have already mentioned, Corgis are cattle dogs; not palace dwellers. To my mind, the very idea of Corgis in a Royal Palace is a symptom of declining moral standards.

Little wonder, then, that so many people turn to drugs and alcohol. I'm not averse to the odd gin and tonic myself, but within reason.

I therefore decided to launch a moral crusade with a view to improving the lot of the working man.

Pugs Not Drugs was born, and I'm happy to say the campaign has been a huge success! (And to think it started off with an inauspicious poster on Jasmine's bedroom wall.) According to the staff member who manages it, just about every street in the UK now has a Pug which they share around as part of a **Neighbourhood Pooch scheme**.

While Off Licenses, Tobacconists, and Big Pharma, have expressed their reservations, not to mention street dealers, the initiative has won the praise of many intellectuals and political leaders the world over, and has now been implemented almost everywhere except North Korea. Sadly, they chose to spend their money on nuclear missiles. I understand there are ongoing diplomatic efforts to show them the error of their ways, and that the American President has also intervened on behalf of my campaign.

I'm not sure of the exact details of these political shenanigans, as I leave all that to my staff. Hope springs eternal, however.

CHAPTER 21

OVER AND ABOVE THE CALL OF DUTY

I have heard it said that if you give enough typewriters to enough monkeys they will eventually turn out the works of Shakespeare. In other words, it is being argued that just about anything can be created by chance alone, over time. Personally, I couldn't disagree more. I believe that my life has purpose with just as much certainty as I know myself to have been appointed by God ... and to be a shining example of my glorious breed.

With this in mind, I felt dutybound to commit some of my life to print for the many of you who are sure to find it fascinating. I say again, a magnanimous gesture on my part, I am sure you will agree. Privilege may have its perks, but rank also comes with responsibility.

To further illustrate this point, I travelled all the way from London to Huddersfield in West Yorkshire just to watch a football match last weekend. Huddersfield Town FC were playing the mighty Manchester United. I'm not a big football fan to be honest (it's all a bit working class for my liking), but in an effort to improve inter-breed relationships, I agreed to attend this game because the team is owned and run by a local Terrier. I think they are also nicknamed the *Yorkshire Terriers*, in fact, and that Huddersfield are the only professional British football team to feature a dog on their club crest.

Although unfancied, the Terriers chalked up a fine 2-1 victory. I was pleased my attendance inspired the home side to raise their game, although I don't plan to attend another one anytime soon. The whole affair was far too noisy and boisterous for my liking.

Also, seeing as it was essentially a diplomatic mission, I didn't like to point out that the large Yorkshire Terrier waving to the children at the side of the pitch was actually a man in a furry suit. Discretion being the part of valour, I bit my lip and kept it to myself. I didn't want to rain on their victory parade.

I had made my point. Wherever Pugs go, good fortune follows.

You may write to me if you wish. My staff will try and respond if they have time. An address can be provided if you would like to purchase merchandise, and request signed photographs, etc. It's all rather a bore, but we all have our crosses to bear.

I hope you feel uplifted for having read about my life. It has been a pleasure — for you almost certainly — but also for me.

Enough for now. Royal duties beckon.

Bonne chance

The Gorgeous Gizmo

www.ingramcontent.com/pod-product-compliance
Lightning Source LLC
Chambersburg PA
CBHW060543030426
42337CB00021B/4412